It's the Little Things!

∽

99 Ways to Create Joy, Health & Happiness

Martie Pineda

ISBN 0692283668
ISBN 13: 9780692283660
Library of Congress Control Number: 2014915697
Martie Pineda, Silver Spring, MD

Table of Contents

Dedication

This book is dedicated to my husband Jerry, and my three sons, Adrian, Jaime and Beau. I dedicate this book to you all for your perseverance during my journey to transformation, and for surviving my sometimes-erratic ways of being.

Thank you for giving me the space to figure *it* out, and for being my guinea pigs in the process—until I could put it all in this book.

Because after all is said and done, it's the little things that make a difference in life and create the joy and happiness we are all striving for!

I love you all with all my heart!

Introduction

This book was inspired by my desire to share the positive things that have made a difference for me. As an adult with ADD and HDD, only recently diagnosed, I have had to *figure it out* on my own, and create ways to make things work for me. What I noticed was that just by applying some little habits or tips or changes, life has become so much better and easier, and it just flowed more and I was happier and more joyful.

Along the way I have done lots of personal development work and I have learned so many life-transforming tools. Some tools have been simple, innocuous things that I might have learned from a magazine article or from observing a friend. Other tools and habits, I have cultivated and honed over the years and I now wear them like a badge of honor. I figured things out in my own time through trial and error.

However I came to acquire my tools over time, I now want to share what I've learned with you. I realize that while great discoveries can be awesome and life-changing, its *the little things* that we do to support ourselves throughout the everyday trials and tribulations that will bring more joy, health and happiness and improve our lives, making them better and richer and more grace filled.

In his book, *The Compound Effect,* Darren Hardy, talks about how doing little things consistently over time creates great and awesome changes and transformation for the long haul. Imagine in a romantic relationship, the gift of a single flower given either daily or weekly or even monthly over the course of a year, or two or ten. Imagine the cumulative affect on the relationship! Apply the same concept to your bank account, your job, your health and you can imagine the benefits over time.

So with the many possibilities in mind, here are 99 ways that can make your life more joyful, healthy, and happy!

Here's to your joy, health & happiness,

Martie

The First Little Thing – The little voice
Little Thing #1

Listen to the Little Voice

Listen to the little voice, the quiet, little voice deep down inside of you, that is constantly trying to give you guidance. You know the one, the quiet, little voice that gets drowned out by the loud and chaotic machinations of daily life. So often, this little knowing and wise voice has no power because we give it away to our friends, family and the media. Slow down, be still and know that you are the ultimate wisdom in your life

Little Things to Care for the Sacred Temple

If you ask most people what would be the most important change they could make to be healthier, happier or more joyful, they would probably say, "eat better!" And while what we eat is very important, I bet you didn't know that you could probably go a few weeks with out eating, while not drinking water for even 3-4 days could potentially create such an imbalance in your body that you could actually become chronically dehydrated and suffer tremendous health consequences and even death.

Water is a magical thing, we drink it, bathe with it, clean with it, play in it, heal with it, it is so essential and life giving, yet it is one of the most under appreciated and under utilized elements in our consciousness.

Little Thing #2

Drink 20 ounces of water

Drink at least twenty ounces of water as soon as you wake up.

Quality water is second only to air to the importance of not only survival, but also great health! Our muscles are made up of about 75% water, blood is 82% water, our lungs are 90% water, even our bones are 25% water. By the time we actually feel thirst, we are already severely dehydrated.

Our brain is about 76% water. Water gets your brain hydrated and functioning optimally to get your day going. Most people reach for coffee before they are even awake. Drinking coffee will actually further dehydrate your body, causing it to lose more water than what is in your cup of coffee—about 20% more! Now you understand why you feel fuzzy sometimes, you may not be hydrating responsibly!

It's also critical to drink water to lose weight. How many times have you been scavenging around for something to eat, and found yourself going through all kinds of snacks only to fill up on a bunch of calorie laden, nutrient void junk, and still felt empty and tired? More than likely you were dehydrated and looking for energy, and thought that by eating you could find the energy you were looking for.

When you are hydrating sufficiently and efficiently you will feel satisfied with less food! You will not have the compulsion to overeat because you are not dehydrated and your body is not looking for energy in the form of carbohydrates and fat!

Drink more water!

For more information on the importance of water, see *Water: For health, for healing, for Life: You're not sick, you're thirsty*, by Dr. F Batmanghelidj

Detox tip:

Squeeze half a lemon or lime into your morning glass of water instead of reaching for coffee. Try starting every day with this simple little cocktail.

The liver produces more enzymes in response to water with lemon than any other food. Water and lemon juice is a great way to start the cleansing process first thing in the morning.

Give your liver a little love, with lemon water every day to thank it for all that it does for you every single day of your life!

Little Thing #3

Hydrate responsibly

In order for your body to get the proper amount of water it needs to function properly we need to drink half of our body weight in ounces of water daily.

Dr. Batmanghelidj, a pioneer in water research states that, "Unintentional Chronic Dehydration (UCD) contributes to and even produces pain and many degenerative diseases that can be prevented and treated by increasing water intake on a regular basis."

Digestion is greatly affected by lack of hydration. Your brain and vital body functions will take whatever water you have in your body, even taking water from your bowels, to keep your body and brain functioning optimally. Of course that can then lead to other issues such as constipation. Water first thing in the morning gets the digestive process going. Water is also very important for the lubrication and flexibility of your joints. Your creaky joints may just be thirsty.

Little Thing #4

Spritz your face!

Spritzing your face with 6.0 ph water throughout the day will hydrate and refresh your skin. Most of us are chronically dehydrated and our facial skin more so from being exposed to the elements all the time. There is nothing more refreshing than taking a mini atomizer (fancy or not) and spraying your face with it during the day. This will moisturize and hydrate your facial skin, and your skin will thank you over time.

Little Thing #5

Drink *sexy water*

Prepare your water with sliced cucumbers, fresh mint, basil, parsley, cilantro or a mix of fresh herbs, sliced limes, sliced lemons, sliced oranges, sliced grapefruit, fresh sliced strawberries, fresh raspberries, blueberries—the possibilities are endless!

Adding fresh, clean fruits, vegetables or herbs to fresh, clean water will not only make it look more appealing and better and fresher tasting, but these foods will actually add vital nutrients to your water.

For ease and convenience, bring home your choice of sexy ingredients, wash them and slice them and put them in a zip lock bag or box and put them in the freezer and then pull them out when you are in a hurry and just add them to your pitcher or bottle of cool water.

Another easy tip: fill your ice cube trays with water and place berries in the individual slots for beautiful tasty ice cubes.

Little Thing #6

Immerse with music

As simple as this sounds, most of us do not take the time to take a relaxing and soul nourishing bath. So leave your cell phone off or in another room. No books or other distracting devices. Just turn on some soothing music and add the nice, hot, soul-soothing water. I like to add some sea salt for extra skin nourishment and relaxation, and it can also help with detoxing.

Little Thing #7

Scrub your body with a *cotton*

How about a little personal daily massage? Using a cotton wash clothe has a completely different effect on the body when used as a tool for creating a soothing massage; it's gentle and natural fibers offer a nurturing effect. Soap it up or use it plain with water; it's a wonderful way to sooth your body after a rough day.

Little Thing #8

Sprinkle Himalayan Pink salt

This is a little big thing actually. Salt is an essential nutrient. Pink Himalayan salt is full of phyto-nutrients and, of course, the life giving mineral sodium. Most of the regular table salt that you purchase at the super market is loaded with sodium chloride, the ingredient that makes salt (an essential nutrient) unhealthy.

Little Thing #9

Eat more carrots

The easiest way to enjoy them is to shred a couple of carrots and sprinkle with lime or lemon juice and pink Himalayan salt and fresh ground pepper. Eating carrots can be simple, delicious and beautiful. If you are feeling particularly adventuresome, add a pile of shredded daikon root and shredded beets. Make three little piles on your salad plate, sprinkle with lemon juice and Himalayan pink salt and present with your main meal. Now you have a lovely rainbow, and have added even more nutritious variety to your plate!

Little Thing #10

Eat and (re-eat) roasted veggies

Use either or a combination of 3 cups of washed and peeled carrots, potatoes, parsnips, beets, brussels sprouts, broccoli or eggplant, etc. Chop the veggies into bite size pieces. Preheat the oven to 400 degrees, coat the veggies with 2 tablespoons of olive oil, sprinkle with salt and pepper and herbs if desired, put in a baking dish or on a tray, and bake for 20 minutes or until golden brown and tender. Or put in a pan and stir and roast until browned and tender and cover and let cook for about 15 to 20 minutes, or until tender. Serve hot or cold. (use olive oil more liberally if desired)

Use the leftover roasted veggies by warming them up in a non-stick pan with a little bit of olive oil; when heated through, scramble a couple of eggs and pour over and lift egg edges to allow the raw egg to flow under to continue to cook. When completely cooked, flip over and sprinkle with cheese, cover with lid to melt, or pop into the broiler for a couple of minutes. Serve with a green salad! AMAZING! And oh so easy!

You could also use the leftover roasted veggies by warming them up in a non-stick pan with a little bit of olive oil and when heated through, add fresh or left over quinoa and 2 or 3 tablespoons of water. Cook over medium heat for about 5 minutes with a lid on, until heated through. Add cheese or cooked meat, chicken or shrimp for a quick meal.

Little Thing #11

Eat more fruit-no brainer!

Fruit is the original fast food. Fruits are so easy, and delicious and simple and nutrient dense! This is one of the best and easiest ways to boost your nutrition and health. Fresh fruit is probably the easiest, then dried fruits and of course frozen. Apples, bananas, pears, oranges are super portable; just wash and eat. Some of the other wonderful varieties require a little more effort, peeling, chopping and refrigeration, and the benefits are so worth the effort. Eat at least two servings a day.

Little Thing #12

Eat real butter!

This is in light of new scientific discoveries that are showing that real butter is actually healthier and safer than vegetable oil preparations made with trans fats or heavily processed vegetable oils. Butter. It's the real thing. Eat it and enjoy it.

Little Thing #13

Make your coffee Sexy-er

Add cinnamon to your coffee, you can either sprinkle it on or add it while you are brewing it. Cinnamon has a plethora of healthy benefits (improves circulation, blood glucose management), plus it has a wonderful aroma when it is heated with your coffee. Cinnamon adds a special sexiness to the already sexy ritual of coffee, *and* its good for you.

Little Thing #14

Eat organic. Period.

Lets face it, there are chemicals and toxins everywhere we look these days. Chemicals make food taste awful and are very toxic and bad for your health. Always wash your vegetables and fruits whether they are organic or not. The benefits of eating organic vegetables and fruits are plentiful; better health, lots of free radical-fighting anti-oxidants, better digestion and lots of phyto-nutrients not found anywhere else. Oh and they taste so much better!

Below is a list of a few vegetables and fruits that are considered the dirty dozen plus; these are the ones you should really consider purchasing organic whenever possible:

Apples
Peaches
Grapes
Strawberries
Celery
Cherry tomatoes
Cucumbers
Hot peppers
Imported nectarines
Potatoes

Martie Pineda

Spinach
Sweet bell peppers
Kale
Collard greens
Summer squash

Little Thing #15

If you can't pronounce it, don't eat it

E Nuff said. Period

Little Thing #16

DO NOT MICROWAVE YOUR FOOD!

I know there's lots of controversial information about this, pro and con. Lets just say that until there is conclusive information that it *wont* harm you, lets just not microwave, OK? Warm up food in small, non-stick pans; add about a tablespoon of water and put a lid on it; and go set the table and get your salad and a glass of good water while your food takes three minutes to heat up. There. Warm, safe and delicious food.

Little Thing #17

Eat steel cut organic oatmeal

Whaaaat? No instant or three minute or rolled oats?!?! Have you ever tried steel cut organic oatmeal?!? It is amazing! Like dessert, if you add dried or fresh fruit, butter, almond milk, or regular milk, honey, maple syrup, nuts or seeds!

So here's the trick: Go to the kitchen, get a pot with a lid, put in ½ a cup of steel cut oats, ½ teaspoon of cinnamon, dash of salt, add 2 cups of water and bring to a boil, stir and turn off heat and put the lid on. Go get ready for your day, and the oatmeal will cook while you are gone. Add your pretties: chopped apples, berries, nuts, seeds, stevia, honey, maple syrup, etc. Enjoy. Put the rest in a container for tomorrow! Makes a great snack too!

Little Thing #18

Sauté your greens

Sauté your greens and then add them to everything! This is a total game changer folks. It's an easy and most delicious way to get your nutrient dense greens in. Purchase them in bags at the super market; super greens-baby chard, spinach and kale; they cook up very easily and quickly, and can be added to ANYTHING—eggs, pasta dishes, quesadillas, pizza, rice, potatoes, macaroni, pasta sauces, soups, casseroles, tuna, sandwiches, etc. The delicious possibilities are endless and add huge dividends in nutrients!

Recipe:
Add a splash of olive oil to a frying pan, add some chopped onion (or not), some chopped garlic (or not) and put your greens in (about 2 packed cups per person, as they reduce in volume very quickly). Stir over medium heat until nicely wilted and fragrant. Sprinkle with pink Himalayan salt and fresh ground pepper. Enjoy as a side dish or add cheese or nuts or seeds and enjoy as a main dish.

Little Thing #19

Eat like your body was an exotic sports car

Think of your body as a high performance vehicle, like a Ferrari. Would you try to run a Ferrari with no fuel or with low quality fuel? I think not!

Eat something nutritious every four hours *before you run out of fuel*! While every four hours may or may not work for everyone, the body will use up what you put into it, so it needs to be "refueled" regularly to work as efficiently as it is designed to. Mind you, it WILL keep working without high quality fuel—until it doesn't! Lack of nutrients causes stress on your body.

Healthy snack ideas: water, nuts, carrots, apples, bananas, oranges, cherries, blueberries, cheese, hard boiled eggs, celery sticks with nut butter, raisins.

Love your body for all the work it does for you!

Little Thing #20

Eat a "Rainbow" every day

Every day your goal is to eat at least five different colors of fruits and/or vegetables. Add one more new fruit or vegetable to your shopping cart a week to expand your palate and nutritional profile.

A serving is only ½ cup. Easy peasy! PS ketchup is not a vegetable.

Little Thing #21

Avoid H.F.C.S. like the plague!

High fructose corn syrup is in so many processed foods, so read all the labels! HFCS is a sweetener that is used in United States food production because it is much cheaper than sugar. There are studies that show that the human body is not designed to process this product. Enough said!

Little Thing #22

Drink your greens daily

Clinical studies have shown that drinking **ONE** green smoothie a day will increase your energy, stamina and recovery very quickly and will fortify you with all kinds of healthy vitamins, minerals, phyto-nutrients and anti-oxidants.

The best way to do this is to cut up your fruits and veggies once a week and refrigerate or freeze them in individual little zip lock bags or freezer containers. Then just pop them into the blender with water, juice, milk, coconut water or yogurt. You can also add protein powder, flax seed, pumpkin seeds, sunflower seeds, hemp seeds, almonds, walnuts, pecans, whatever you like. Another option is to use powdered greens and powdered protein formulas.

Healthy and delicious smoothie Recipes:

In a blender cup, place
1 large handful of fresh, packed spinach, kale, or chard leaves or a mixture
1 cup of fresh or frozen pineapple or strawberries or mangos or blueberries or bananas
Juice of ½ a lemon
1 cup of water or coconut water or juice or nut milk

Stevia to taste, I prefer pure organic stevia (or honey, agave or maple syrup)

Option: ½ cup of yogurt (I prefer plain greek style)

When you get really adventuresome add some seeds or nuts! Whirl in blender until smooth and enjoy!

Little Thing #23

Use the good dishes

Stop using disposable plates, cups and utensils!! Studies allege that plastic products emit gasses that permeate our food and drink. Not to mention the burden they place on our landfills. Real plates and glasses add so much to the dining experience, just like real forks and napkins. Eating and nourishing our bodies, is a special occasion, and who is more special and deserving than you? When is more important than right now? You deserve a real glass, plate and fork. So use the good dishes! And if you don't have any, get some!

Exercise is Essential for Health & Happiness

"If we don't take care of our bodies, where are we going to live?"—Dr. Wayne Dyer

Embrace exercise, it is what will keep your body strong and viable. Your body is the shelter for your soul and the vehicle to carry you around on your earth journey. If you can exercise, consider it a gift and a privilege.

When I was very young, I walked into the dressing room at the YWCA and there next to her locker was this very elegant woman finishing getting dressed as I groaned, as I threw my gym bag on the bench, I huffed out a grunt about having to, "do this again!!!" She looked at me and smiled, "Yep, we have to do it until we die!" I looked at her in semi-disbelief and it hit me, "Oh yeah, huh?" At the time, I still didn't really embrace exercise. For years, I still exercised and grumbled and complained and felt like exercise was more of a punishment. Work!

Today at my age, I love the fact that I CAN EXERCISE! Last year at 57, I parachuted twice, once over the farms of Northern Virginia and once over the Island of Oahu.

My Mom, God rest her soul, was incapacitated at the tender age of 44. She could hardly walk, but she would do little stretches from her wheelchair and isometrics in her bed. God love you mom!!

Whether you dance, walk, jog, bicycle, garden, do tai chi, or yoga, or whatever—just move! At least 30 minutes, 5 days a week!

We need to exercise, until we don't need our bodies anymore; it's essential and it can be fun! Consult with your Dr. before you start any exercise program.

Little Thing #24

Commune for 10

For those who think *exercise* is a nasty word, walking just 10 minutes a day will make a huge difference in revving your metabolism. Walking will help to connect you with nature and allow you to take in fresh air and clear your mind.

Walking increases your energy, activates your lymphatic system, and oxygenates your blood. And it's quick, easy and you don't need any special equipment or memberships.

Make walking a part of your regular schedule, put it on your calendar.

Little Thing #25

Plank gut strength

The Plank is a marvelous exercise that increases body and core strength while very quickly flattening the stomach. A few minutes of this powerful exercise will reap incredible benefits if done correctly and consistently.

The benefits are multiple: build upper body, core, back, shoulder, abdominal, and even leg strength with this one exercise.

How to do the plank: Lie face down on a firm surface, come up on elbows with upper arms flat on floor, hands folded or flat on floor, elbows below shoulders, come up on toes. Hold body firmly and keep stomach tight, facing the floor. And count, one one thousand…two one thousand….

Hold the pose as long as you can, while you breathe. Start by holding the pose at least 10 seconds and do five sets, build up from there to do five sets of 60 seconds.

One or two minutes is a long time with this exercise. Be sure to keep your body nice and straight and strong while you do it. Go as long as you can and release and rest. Repeat five times.

Don't despair, I promise this one "little thing" will reap awesome results!

Little Thing #26

Do a 4-minute workout!

Try Tabata, it is an Interval Exercise! 20 seconds of high intensity (your choice) alternated with 10 seconds of rest for four minutes. That's it!

Have you ever wondered how little you could get by with in an exercise program? Well here is your answer!

Tabata is a Japanese exercise system that works in 4 minutes! Yes siree, 4 minutes-ideally twice a day, but you will see a difference even if you only do it once a day.

You can choose the high intensity exercises and build on that. Yoga, calisthenics, resistance moves, Latin dance, Hip Hop, there is no limit to what type of exercise you can incorporate here. The most basic could look like walking/running in place for 20 seconds and then standing for 10 seconds. The important thing is to do it!!! So do it!!

Little Thing #27

Do yoga to reduce stress, lose weight, & build

strength

There is a misconception that Yoga is for spiritual types or for people who can't do other more rigorous types of exercise. What is real about Yoga is that you can create great stress reduction at the same time you create awesome physical strength and flexibility. And that is not all: flexibility is also a state of mind. When the body is able to move and flow with ease, guess what happens to the thinking?!?

There is a series of exercises called the Sun Salutation. It is a series of exercises that also has its own variations depending on the level of the student. Google Sun Salutation or visit a local yoga studio and try it out!

Detox for life

Everything needs to be cleaned out eventually and our bodies are no different. Have you ever given a thought about what your liver, lungs, heart or pancreas must look like? Well think about it. For as long as you have been alive, your organs have been at it, 24/7, with no break or opportunity to take a rest.

Detox is not a new phenomenon. In the "Olden Days," many religions had holy days where you would fast for a period of time to some degree, some more rigorous than others. Many people have opted away from these customs and traditions. Some ancient cultures also fasted for health reasons.

Detoxing is now being embraced as a healthy way to give your vital organs a rest from all the toxins that they process daily. It's kind of like giving your body an oil change, only your filter (your organs) stays in place while the oil (your food intake) is changed. Many westerners will go from the typical taxing diet full of fats; processed, sugary, heavy carbohydrate fare; and animal proteins; to a much lighter diet of fresh vegetable or fruit juices or foods that are very easy to digest. This gives the body's organs a chance to rest and heal and have the opportunity to clear and clean out the gunk that clogs and slows them down.

A detox program is as individual as the person doing it. There are different levels of detox, just as there are different levels of exercise for everyone. It is not a one size fits all for sure. There are many books out there and probably it would be best to confer with a health coach to help guide you through this process. You can however, do little things to detox daily.

Little Thing #28

Stop drinking soft drinks. Just STOP!

According to Dr. Otto Warburg, in his 1931 studies, he found that cancer thrived in an acidic, oxygen-depleted environment. Consuming acid causing foods and beverages is the root cause of all degenerative disease. Most carbonated soft drinks measure about 3.0 ph. Which makes them very acidic.

Little Thing #29

Go Meatless Monday or Tuesday or . . .

Eat less meat. Make a conscious choice to have a meatless meal or two or more; either daily, weekly or even monthly. Studies show that eating less animal products will have a positive effect on your health. It's also a great way to cut back on fat, expense, stress on your digestive system, ecological stress; there are myriad great reasons to consider this "little thing." Plus it gives you an opportunity to try other options on the menu of life!

Little Thing #30

Skip breakfast, lunch or dinner...intentionally

This is a great way to give your body a rest. Only it has to be done intentionally so you are supporting your body with plenty of water and or fresh juice. And when you do eat, eat with consciousness and eat nutritiously. This mini fasting has been shown to be very beneficial and can be a one meal, two meal or even full day fast. Again intentionality is key.

Little Thing #31

Curb chemicals

Everything our bodies take in, from the air we breath to the water we drink, to the food we eat and whatever we use on our skin and hair is being processed by our fabulous hard working organs. Doesn't it make sense that we would want to expose ourselves and our temples and those of our loved ones to the least amount of toxic chemicals possible?

There are many wonderful natural cleaners out there these days. And in addition to those awesome products there are the old stand bys. Vinegar, baking soda, borax powder, lemon juice and water work wonders.

Little Thing #32

Tune them out!

If you are stressed or feeling anxious about the way things are in the world, stop watching! Detach with an axe from all the sources that are flooding your world with bad and toxic news! Focus instead on the actual world in front of you. Your immediate world is safe and secure and can be a joyful place. Focus on the good things, and say a prayer for those things that are out of your control.

Nutritional Supplements

Lets face it folks, our food supply is not what it used to be. Our farms' soil is depleted of nutrients. I heard somewhere that we need to eat five times the amount of broccoli to get the same amount of nutrients that we used to get. Okay, even if we need to eat twice the amount, that's a lot of broccoli! Most of us are not eating or drinking nearly the minimal amount of our daily requirement of vegetables or fruits.

The fact is, stress is at an all time high for a lot of people. When we are stressed out, our bodies consumes more nutrients to run the body, especially for people who live in metropolitan areas. A regular diet with "normal" nutrients is just the tip of the iceberg (pardon the pun), and you should absolutely eat the best natural and fresh food possible, but its just not going to be enough. Is it any wonder the United States is number 38 on the list of most healthy countries right behind Cuba, and on par with Serbia?

Little Thing #33

Magnesium

Magnesium is crucial to bone formation, it helps with healing, it is an anti-viral, anti-fungal, anti-bacterial and it helps calcium to assimilate. It also helps to calm you and to support your sleep. And so much more!

Little Thing #34

Vitamin C

Vitamin C is a super vitamin. It reinforces the immune system and helps to resist viral and bacterial infections. It also helps with collagen production and tissue repair. It assists the liver with detoxification. And so much more!

Little Thing #35

Vitamin B-12

Vitamin B Complex is important for metabolic functions and tissue healing, it helps to release energy from carbohydrates. When you're under a lot of stress, this is a crucial nutrient that supports the nervous system. And so much more!

Little Thing #36

Calcium

Calcium is important for bone health, joint health, has calming properties, and it supports quality sleep. And lots, lots more!

Little Thing #37

Vitamin D

The best source of Vitamin D is sunshine, and Westerners currently are suffering Vit D deficiency in increasing numbers, possibly because we are all covered up and/or slathered with sunscreen. Vitamin D is necessary for bone health and absorption of calcium and phosphorus. Lack of this vital nutrient can cause rickets, a bone deformity in children.

Little Thing #38

Take some Vitamin "H"

I learned about this very, very important nutrient at my health coaching school, the Institute of Integrative Nutrition. Vitamin "H" is only found in "home cooked" food. And I highly recommend it, because nothing really compares to it, except perhaps your mom or grandmom's home cooked food. There are many benefits to this nutrient. You can control, where the food comes from, how it is stored, how old it is, how it is prepared and seasoned. It is also a great way to economize and save money on eating out.

Do your best to eat in as much as possible or do your own version of "take out" from home.

Personal Care & Self-Love

Few of us get the kind of TLC (tender loving care) we need or deserve. So often we do not get our share of personal care because it is not even in our subconscious thinking to do so. Women in particular are apt to omit themselves from "the list". It is your own responsibility to take care of yourselves. When your vessel is filled, it is easier to fill the vessels of those who love you and who depend on you!

Here is a short list to get you started.

Little Thing #39

Get a massage

And schedule another one on a regular basis. Touch is one of those things that we just don't get enough of. And massage can fill that bill beautifully and then some.

There are many different types of massage: Swedish, Aromatherapy, Hot stone, Deep tissue, Shiatsu, Thai, Reflexology, Sports, Back massage, Detox, Relaxation, Lomi lomi. Take the plunge and experiment. You won't get it wrong!

Massage can help with detox, with stress management, with relaxation, with skin treatment, with weight loss, with just plain indulgent self-love.

You do not need a reason to get a massage, you deserve one because you are.

Little Thing #40

M is for Manicure & P is for Pedicure

Nicely groomed hands are a huge boon to a put-together professional. It is really not an option. When you go get a manicure, you will be doing a two-fer. You can give yourself the gift of self-care and get your nails done at the same time.

It is such a great feeling to look down at your hands and have them look nice because your nails are "done".

It's a little thing that pays huge dividends! Get a manicure, because you are worth it!

And one of life's special little pleasures is to have a skillful nail technician take your dry, tired feet and remove all the crusty skin off of them, then proceed to give you a fabulous foot and leg massage followed by painting your little toenails a gorgeous color of your choice (or not, guys—a simple buff for a smooth natural finish is fine). Then aptly fit you with those brightly colored flip-flops to prance out of the salon in!

It's a small price to pay to feel like royalty!

Little Thing #41

F is for Fabulous Facials

One cannot appreciate a facial until one has had one. It is one of those mysteries of life. Why do I need a facial? My face is clean. Facials are done by skilled estheticians (depending on where you go).

These people are highly trained and skilled in delivering a wonderful facial and upper body massage, coupled with skin cleansing, perhaps a deep pore cleansing, depending on your needs, and then a delicious cleansing, moisturizing or toning mask, again all customized depending on your needs and preferences.

The facial will be finished off with a delectable toner and moisturizer, perhaps some eye cream and facial serums to plump and nourish your skin. The benefits of such a treatment can range from just feeling relaxed from completely disconnecting from the real world, to looking and feeling rejuvenated and revived, and feeling like you can tackle anything now that your face is looking its absolute best!

Little Thing #42

A is for Acupuncture

Acupuncture is an ancient healing art that is beneficial for many things, in particular relaxation and stress relief. The effect is feeling very calm and peaceful afterwards. I highly recommend it when stakes are high and you are feeling stressed. You can not imagine the amazing benefits until you have experienced it.

Little Thing #43

Find your Tribe

Sometimes life throws us a curve ball and we have no idea how to deal with it. Sometimes we can handle it. Sometimes we can pretend we are handling it. Sometimes we just drop the ball because it is just too hard to handle it.

When this happens, there are groups out there that meet to give each other support. There is Moral support, Group support; all kinds of support out there waiting for you.

Reach out and connect, there is nothing like knowing you are not alone in your misery and that there are others who have gone through what you are going through and found the light at the end of the tunnel.

Little Thing #44

Go A.W.O.L!

Take a personal day....OFF! And really be off!

Sometimes we just need to take a day to just disconnect and do whatever we want- all by our selves. Stop, shop and eat and do whatever our little hearts desire.

Make a date with yourself to treat yourself to fun and/or relaxation. Make an appointment to treat your self to any or ALL of the treatments above or just take a day to slack off!

Everybody deserves a day off—just like Ferris Bueller!

Little Thing #45

Start the day with a "Thank you!"

Connecting with yourself and the Universe, or divine Creator or what-or-whomever you deem to be in charge, is important as you open your eyes to greet the day. Gratitude for all that is good and available in your life is a great way to start the day, and it can help to take the edge off of whatever may not be going exactly as you would wish it to be.

Thank you. It's short, sweet and doable. Try it, and see if it does'nt make life just a little bit more gracious.

Little Thing #46

"No."

No is a complete sentence. This "little thing" will give you a lot of freedom if you use it! There is no need to give an explanation as to why your response is no. "No" is a complete answer. The more you practice it, the easier it gets. People may not like it, but they'll get over it. I used to feel compelled to explain and even apologize, whenever I didn't want to do something. Now I know I can just say "No"!

Little Thing #47

Plan a "fling thing"

Schedule regular date nights with your significant other. Connecting with the people you care about is tantamount to personal care. No more explanation is needed other than that you need time that is dedicated just for the two of you to connect over anything outside of kids and home affairs. Surprise your significant other with a special night out—just because!

Little Thing #48

Celebrate a weekly family day or night

What a concept! Connecting with the people who are supposed to matter the most. Once a week have breakfast, brunch, lunch, snack, coffee, tea or dinner, whatever! If it can't happen in person, do a Skype or Google Hangout reunion! This is the technological age! Getting together can't be that hard.

Little Thing #49

Learn your *Color*

The Color Code, www.colorcode.com, is a free personality test offered by Dr. Taylor Hartman, a psychologist. This information absolutely transformed my life and my husband's! By learning what my motivation in life is and what my husband's is, so much was demystified and each of us now has a completely different appreciation for each other. We are also more tolerant and patient with each other. Huge little thing!

Little Thing #50

Learn your and your partner's Love Languages

In *The Five Love Languages: the secret to love that lasts*, Gary Chapman talks about how all of us have a way that we interpret love. And if you know how you interpret love and how your partner interprets love then things can run so much more smoothly. When we have our love needs met, there's less confusion and more happiness and joy in our lives! No need to guess what you or they need to be happy!

Little Thing #51

Parent compassionately

Dr. Shefali Tsabary has written what I believe is a master-piece and global change agent book in *The Conscious Parent: Transforming ourselves, empowering our children*. I only wish it had been written sooner. I only recently heard of this book, and I used some of what I heard on my 38-year-old son, and it was awe-inspiring what I experienced!

Compassionate, authentic and fearless are powerful ways of being, especially with your children.

Little Thing #52

Model reflective behavior

Whatever we do or say is what our children will do or say. Our children are our biggest fans, and there is no bigger love affair than that of a parent and their child. So why would we be anything less than model, stellar citizens when our most precious assets are sitting front and center watching us?

This would actually apply to anyone else you care about; partner, lover, employees, and friends. Be the best you that you can be in any given moment.

Little Thing #53

When your kids talk, listen; *really listen*

As a parent, I know from experience (I didn't say great experience) that sometimes we have a way of listening to our kids, and wanting to problem solve or fix or sleuth our conversations with our kids, instead of just hearing what they are saying and listening to them, listening to their hearts, and what they are really saying.

When our kids talk to us, it is important that we stop everything and really listen. When we do that, they will share themselves with us, which is why we had them in the first place.

Little Thing #54

Invest in YOU!

Personal development is the best investment you can make in yourself and for those around you. Who we are is what we send out into the universe. People ask me all the time, what my secret is to my long and happy marriage. After thinking about it, I can attribute it to my personal development efforts. Through the wisdom and tools that I have garnered from many, and I do mean *many*, self improvement and transformational programs, I can honestly say that the me that steps out these days is a completely different person than the one that came back to the United States 13 years ago. This transformation, and self-work, translates daily into more authenticity, kindness, joy, love and knowingness. And I know that without a doubt, the ripple I send out is making a difference to those I meet.

Little Thing #55

Reach out and say, "Hey!"

Have you ever noticed how time flies? Before you know it months, then years pass by and you have not talked to your aunts, uncles, cousins or some of your friends. Schedule a call once a week for 10 minutes just to reach out and connect. The person you connect with will feel so special that you took the time. And you will feel good because you took the time. You can even leave a message; it is the act that makes the difference. What is that saying, "The road to hell is paved with good intentions?"

Little Thing #56

Pause...before you speak

Before you say *anything*—and these days, write or post any-thing—ask yourself these three questions:
Is it true?
Is it kind?
Is it necessary?

You may find, you may not need to say anything after all.

Little Thing #57

Be kind

This doesn't require any explanation other than we as humans have incredible potential for being really loving and caring and kind beings. And somehow, some of us have been distracted and have lost that capacity along the way. I believe that it is there waiting quietly to be unleashed and shared in amazing and unbridled ways. We just have to let it out.

I am declaring with this "little thing" that we all be more kind and do more kind acts more frequently!

Little Thing #58

Who I am today is . . .?

The power of declaration! Have you ever noticed how we can talk ourselves into almost anything? Well we can, and I am inviting you to talk yourself into something that you want to be—not someone you don't want to be.

Anyone can call themselves a loser, dummy, jerk, etc. What if you could choose to be smart, honorable, gentle, compassionate, kind, courageous, joyful, friendly, loving? Getting the picture?

So today, before you go out the door to meet your day, *Who* are you choosing to be?

Managing the Stress Monster

Stress is an inevitable thing. It can be a good thing and help us get moving and make changes for the better. And it can become a chronic way of living or just surviving.

The good news is that there are many ways to deal with stress and it's a bunch of "little things" that we can do to make that happen!

Little Thing #59

Dump your junk!

Start the day Journaling and do a brain dump. A lovely tool that I recently started using is something called "morning papers." You write three pages that you start off with 10 things you are grateful for and then you just dump your brain and your emotions onto the pages. I am able to put out things that I am frustrated with, issues that I have not resolved completely, all kinds of junk that takes up space in my thoughts. I have found that it really helps calm my monkey mind and then allows me to be able to meditate more productively after I unload on my morning papers journal.

Little Thing #60

Talk to God and be still to hear the response

There are all different ways to approach prayer and meditation. The best thing is to find a way that works for you. There is no one correct way. The goal is to quiet your mind so you can hear yourself clearly. There is Transcendental Meditation, group meditation, guided meditation, musical meditation; there is the meditation that you experience when you run or practice yoga. My personal favorite is when I stop at a red light and I close my eyes for a minute and just get quiet. I find I can think about what I have on my mind and "put it out there".

Meditation is really about finding a time and space to give the mind a break, a space to hear yourself think. It is an opportunity to stop the incessant chatter that goes on around us and allow for the quiet voice within to be heard. This is particularly important these days with so much to distract us. Finding a time and space to connect with yourself is a gift that only we can give to ourselves.

Little Thing #61

Spritz the sheets

There are many different calming aromas that help to manage stress, my favorite, and one of the most effective, is lavender oil. To help with restful sleep, spritz lavender essential oil (diluted with purified water) onto bed sheets before sleep; it is very soothing and relaxing.

Little Thing #62

Breathe 4.7.8

Breathing can be a very powerful relaxant and stress man-ager, especially when practiced mindfully. I learned this breathing exercise from Dr. Andrew Weil. You do four sets for a total of one minute. Start out sitting when you first attempt this practice, it takes awhile to train the body.

First, blow out all the air in your lungs powerfully with a whoosh sound. Then inhale for **4** seconds, hold for **7** seconds, then exhale forcefully with an open mouth for **8** seconds. Repeat four times. You may feel a little light-headed at first, but after practicing it awhile it will start to feel quite lovely and soothing.

Little Thing #63

Supplements to calm your body & mind

Calcium and magnesium have a very calming effect on the nervous system. Calcium is proven to help with improving sleep.

B-12 vitamins are also very helpful to manage stress, they are also very soothing to the nervous system. Ask your Dr. what supplements are best for you.

Little Thing #64

Laugh!

I always say that laughter is the best medicine. Taking a laugh break is a great way to diffuse a stressful situation. Surf funny videos online or keep a file of jokes or silly videos handy so you can enjoy a hearty, belly-jiggling laugh when you need it.

Little Thing #65

Work it out!

Physical activity is a great stress reliever. Yoga, walking, calisthenics, dancing, running, cycling, it is all good and good for you.

Check with your dr. before you start any program.

Little Thing #66

Eat chocolate; it's a real super food

Dark chocolate is one of the top ten super foods. (Is there any other kind of chocolate besides super?) Not only is it delicious, it releases hormones that make you feel better, it has awesome nutrients and awesome anti-oxidants.

Little Thing #67

Repeat "All is well" Repeat

This little mantra has helped me numerous times when I have been crazed with either fear or stress. I just repeat it over and over and over and after awhile I start to feel calm and collected. Sometimes, I repeat silently in my head, other times I whisper it under my breath and other times I chant it out loud. It all depends on my mood. And the situation.

Your Sanctuary & *Space of Grace*

Your home is your sanctuary; clutter has no place in a space of grace. As you will find, creating a space of grace does not have to be complicated or difficult; it's the little things that will make it so.

Little Thing #68

Pitch for *Grace*

Pitch what you don't need or love. After a while we all start to amass "stuff" and it starts to feel as if our stuff *owns* us. If your stuff is not beautiful and you are not happy with how it looks or it does not serve a purpose, sell it, donate it, give it away or pitch it. You will feel so light and free in your new space.

I was recently inspired by how restful and minimal a hotel room is, so I did exactly what I am instructing you to do! My new bedroom looks like a Five-star hotel room, and I love it!!!

Little Thing #69

Light it up!

Have you ever been to a place or room where there was just not enough light? It was difficult to see and even uncomfortable to be in. Maybe the wattage of the bulb was inadequate, or there were not enough lamps or light sources? Illuminate every room with at least three to four light sources.

Lighting is a crucial element in a space and it can make or break your experience in it. When in doubt, bring in extra lamps or raise the wattage. Illumination will create such a difference in your space, making it more inviting and livable.

Little Thing #70

Bring nature indoors

Beautify your home with cut flowers. There is nothing like real flowers to add beauty, life and joy to a space, even if it is one lovely rose. Pick them up at the grocery store, when you pick up your groceries.

And bring live plants into your home and office. Real plants add life and oxygen to your space. Pick a species that need minimal care. Diffused lighting works for most and less watering is better than overwatering. My expertise on the matter: If the soil is dry-ish, water the plant. And don't forget the tray to catch excess water drainage!

Little Thing #71

Give it a glow!

Candles add such a beautiful glow and energy to almost any occasion.

Use the ones that are unscented and drip-less, they might cost a little more; but believe me, that is one little thing you will want to do to alleviate other messy problems later. Do not get the scented candles, as a lot of them are toxic and noxious. And don't forget the pretty candleholders while you're at it.

When my boys were little, I would sometimes have a candlelit dinner. It would make an otherwise ordinary dinner into something special. I know it created a special memory for them.

Candles during your bath create an ambiance of luxury and pampering, and if you don't deserve it, who does?

Little Thing #72

Sleep like *Royalty*, why not?

Great sheets and bedspreads, will they help you sleep better? Maybe they will and maybe they won't. But they will make your bedroom feel and look better and that will make you feel better, and isn't that what a sanctuary is supposed to do?

Fabulous luxury linens are available at a fraction of the cost at discount outlets, so why not splurge?

Little Thing #73

Leave only the essentials

Your bedroom is your true sacred sanctuary. This is the space where you go to restore yourself.

A good friend of mine enlightened me on the purpose of a bedroom, "The bedroom is used for two things: one is sleeping and the other, well, is done in the bed and it's not sleeping." You get the point.

Less is more in the case of a bedroom: a bed, a couple of night stands, a couple of lamps, chest of drawers, dresser. Period.

Keeping business, bills, and all other extraneous and stressful things out of the bedroom is important so that we can keep our focus on restful, restorative and wonderful sleep.

Having a desk in your bedroom is taboo, this means there is work in the sacred sanctuary of your sleeping, resting space. Your brain is working even when it is supposed to be sleeping. No desk in the bedroom!

I recently redid my bedroom. More accurately, I edited it. Yes, edited. I took out half of the furnishings, accessories and even half of my clothing articles! I love it!!

Without the clutter and extra stuff, your bedroom space will become more restful, more spacious, more peaceful. LESS is definitely more.

Little Thing #74

Hooks on doors, nothing on floors

This is an awesome little thing for people who don't like to hang things up. There are all kinds of cool things available to put on the inside and outside of your doors for things like: coats, hats, purses, shoes, robes, pants, dresses, shirts, pajamas etc. Keeps things off the floor and bed and furniture!

Note: Do not put these hooks and things on the outside of your door in the bedroom or the bedroom walls.

Little thing #75

Hamper the bedroom clutter

A hamper in the bedroom helps to contain clutter and transport laundry more easily. And if you play your cards right, you might even encourage your partner to use the hamper if they want their laundry done too!

Little thing #76

Appreciate the beauty

Look for the beauty in everything around you, the world is full of it. Look for it and you will find it.

Little Thing #77

Soothe your soul

Anytime you can, play music while you are at home. Music can be therapeutic and inspiring. It can lift your spirit and inspire you.

Little thing #78

Turn'*em* all off!

Some of us have been programmed to have on some kind of noise-making device out of habit: a television, music, iTunes, a movie. Sometimes it is good to not have any noise or music or even conversation. The older I get the more I love the golden sound of silence. Quiet is soothing and healing sometimes. Enjoy peace and quiet.

Oh, and that would include silencing the "peanut gallery" in our heads as well.

Little Thing #79

A tidy bed equals a tidy head

It occurred to me recently, that if people made their bed that somehow they would start their day with a little more order and when they returned to it at the end of the day, things would just be a little more orderly and calmer.

This is a theory from someone who has learned to manage her own Attention Deficit disorder.

If you are in the camp of the non-bed makers, I encourage you to try to at the very least pull the sheets, blankets and bedspread up to the meet the pillows every morning and see if anything shifts around more peacefulness, and a more calming environment at the end of the day.

Little Thing #80

Get your ZZZZ's please!

Sleeping at least six to eight uninterrupted hours a night is crucial to good health and happiness. If you are not getting quality sleep it's hard to be cheerful or healthy or productive.

Sleep is when the body regenerates and rebuilds itself. This is a time of crucial healing and repair. Not just physically, and on a cellular level, but also mentally and emotionally. Without this crucial downtown, the body will get off balance very quickly and start to decline.

The *Annals of Internal Medicine* report (Fall 2012) in a study by University of Chicago researchers, found that the biology of fat cells is actually altered with sleep deprivation. After just four days of less sleep (from 8.5 hours to 4.5 hours), fat cells became less sensitive to insulin, a condition related to both diabetes and obesity. In spite of the fact that the body actually burns more calories during waking hours, other studies showed that food preferences also shifted to include more carbohydrates, thus adding to the weight gain syndrome.

Little Thing #81

Create a sanctuary for sleep & sex

In an ideal world, we are spending about a third of our life in our bed asleep—if we are lucky! To get your best sleep, make your bedroom a sleeping sanctuary by investing in the best mattress you can afford and a great pillow. Beautiful, soft sheets will make your sleep so much more enjoyable and restful.

Your bedroom needs to be cool and dark when you sleep, ideally the room temperature should be on the cool side, 68 degrees or even a little less for those who give off lots of energy.

No lights should be shining into the space, especially blue lights, like from a television, cellular phone or DVR etc. Somehow the brain picks up this type of light and it interferes with our sleep quality. Cover windows completely to keep out the light.

The same goes for noise, our brain is constantly vigilant as to what is going on, even when we are not aware of it. So its important that noise is kept to a minimum for us to get our optimal rest.

Little Thing #82

Evict noisy intruders

Leave noise-making devices outside of the bedroom while you sleep. None of us are indispensible, no matter how important or big our jobs or purposes are. I promise you, we will all make our grand exit eventually and when we do, someone will step in and takeover for us. So leaving your cellular phone on mute, or preferably in another room while you get your much needed and much deserved rest is okay. Really.

If you do need to listen for some loved ones or other important calls, most smart phones have a setting that will allow for some rings to come through while silencing all others. Use this setting for nighttime (and also when you need to get stuff done with out interruptions).

Tip: Leave the cellular in the bathroom on silent, still close but not within reach.

Note: It is a lot healthier to not sleep with our powerful cellular devices on our nightstands, right next to our heads and brains.

PS: Noisy intruders goes for children and pets too.

Little Thing #83

Use a "No Frills" alarm clock

I know this seems so obvious, but some people don't have an alarm clock because they use their cellular or I Phone for everything. The problem is that the phone is now in the room with them while they are trying to get their rest.

A simple no frills battery and electric source alarm clock with no fancy LED lighting on it is the key here. A clock radio would be optimal so you can have great music to ease you into the day.

The only purpose of this clock is to wake you up so that you can sleep soundly until its time to wake up.

Little Thing #84

Prepare for your date with the *"Sandman"*

In today's fast-paced world, routine is tricky. There is so much going on and no one wants to miss anything. Ideally, we wouldn't even sleep at all if we could get away with it. But, we all need to have a regular bedtime so our inner biology can regenerate, repair and regroup itself consistently. Everything would be so hunky dory, right? Well, if we cannot have a regular routine, we could at least create a regular bedtime ritual to prepare us for our very important date with the sandman.

Rituals can help us unwind and ease us into preparation to turn off the day and go into slumber and rest mode.

Some people like to take a shower. I highly recommend this, it takes off the grunge of the day and allows you to drift off to sleep, clean and free of the energies you have been exposed to all day long, plus you are nice and fresh. Brush and floss the pearly whites. I heard once that oral health is tied to cardiac health. Not taking any chances on that. Cleanse and moisturize your face, and ladies remove your makeup.

Wear clean and comfortable pajamas; birthday suits are a good option too. BUT DON'T, I repeat DON'T just fall in with your clothes on! Some people like to read, and if you do, don't read a "page turner," (this includes FB) because the last thing you want to do is get sucked in and then you can't put it down and go to sleep. Bedtime is a good time to read something inspirational, sending you off to sleep on a positive note. Sweet dreams!

Little Thing #85

Recite the ABC's

Whether you are the lucky kind who hits the pillow and goes out, or has to settle in for a few minutes to get comfortable or you have trouble falling asleep, the ABC's of gratitude is a wonderful tool to create peace and wonder in everyone, as we drift off to sleep with a positive mental attitude. List things you're grateful for alphabetically, such as, A is for Attitude; I am grateful for my husband's great attitude. B is for Bedroom; I am grateful for my beautiful and restful Bedroom.

C is for. . . you get the picture....

It is a lovely way to remember all the wonderful things to be grateful for!

Little Thing #86

Nap!!!

Linda Kavelin Popov, Cofounder of *The Virtues Project* and author of *Pace of Grace,* encourages a 20 minute break after 4-6 hours of work. Lay down with a small blanket and either close your eyes and drift off for a nap or read something for pleasure or close your eyes and meditate. The point is to give your body a complete break and rest for 20 minutes to refresh and regroup.

This break actually helps to create a phenomenal bounce back effect, creating lots of energy and stamina to make the rest of the day so much more productive (note how babies and toddlers look so refreshed and come back happy and bouncy after a nap).

The Time Warp

If there is one thing I know about, it's how elusive time can be and how much I have struggled to get myself on some kind of time management program. I personally suffer from time "warpitis". I have used just about every tool there is. So I have plenty of "little things" to share on this topic!

Little Thing #87

Sort mail right next to the recycle bin

Sorting through the mail next to the recycle bin is one of the most ingenious tips I have ever come across and I would be remiss if I didn't pass it on. Pick up your mail and stand (or sit) right next to the recycle bin and pitch all the dead wood—no pun intended. Then proceed to take the mail to its final destination: a desk, basket or drawer or file.

Little Thing #88

Shop online

You can buy almost anything online and have it delivered right to your door. You can buy clothing, groceries, auto parts, autos, shoes, office supplies—anything. Save time, money, aggravation and wear-and -tear on you and your car. You can even have gifts delivered to their destination with no muss or fuss.

Little Thing #89

Automate

If you haven't automated your monthly bills, please stop everything and do this one thing that will revolutionize your life!! If the bills pay themselves every month, you don't have to do it. Brilliant. This is a **huge** little thing! And a huge boon to managing your time!

Little Thing #90

Schedule electronic greetings

This is the coolest thing! There are several electronic greeting card companies with different personalities. Find one that suits you and sign up. Then every quarter or so go through your calendar and schedule the cards for the next few months, at the same time schedule the phone calls you need to make on your calendar so you don't forget to call the people that you care about on their special day—and if you do, at least the card is in their email!

Little Thing #91

Disable the pings & dings

Cancel all the annoying sounds that come from your appliances that work against you working and focusing and being productive! In their place, set up a reminder two or three times a day when you will check your phone, cutting out needless distractions and annoyances. This one little thing will create oodles of productivity and give you back your day.

Little Thing #92

Remove your cells

There is nothing more distracting or crazy making than your cell phone or cell phones, ringing or buzzing when you are trying to get work done; even if you are determined or controlled enough to not pick it up, it still disrupts your train of thought and concentration. Just silence it and put it out of sight (and, out of mind).

Little Thing #93

Review tomorrow's schedule - tonight

Before you wrap up your day, review tomorrow's schedule and determine what things are going to contribute to your personal vision. Ideally, there are about two or three things that you can come up with that will further your cause. Anything that gets done after that is just a bonus!

Little Thing #94

Set timers and reminders for yourself

This little thing has been a game changer for me. Becoming accountable and on time is a big deal for me. Being on time shows you are respectful of the people you are meeting and of your hosts. I personally have to set multiple reminders for myself. I have a tendency to just become so in the moment that time almost stops! So I set my appointments in my smart phone and set timers with reminders to keep me on task! In the kitchen I have other timers and alarms. Being on time is a sign of integrity.

Little Thing #95

Do "IT" first

Sometimes the most important thing on our list is a toss up between seeming emergencies and the thing that will make our dreams come true.

Do what is most important to you *FIRST*, before the phone starts ringing, and people start knocking at your door, and all the other "emergencies" start cropping up. You may have to get up earlier to do this.

This "Little thing" will help you to fulfill on your life goals.

Little Thing #96

Ask yourself, "How important is it?"

When something sets you off and you start to feel agitated, or angry or resentful, STOP. Check inside and see what is really causing this emotional upheaval (Remember Little Thing #1). Ask yourself if the thing you're stressing about is worth giving up your power and peacefulness? So the question to ask yourself is, "How important is it?" You can either attach yourself to your expectation, or you can let it go.

Little Thing #97

Don't answer every ring or ping or knock

Don't be a slave to your cell phone, landline or doorbell. Your life and your dreams are more important. If its important enough, they will leave a message and you can return the message later—preferably when you have scheduled time to return calls and messages.

Little Thing #98

Schedule travel & parking time

Make time for the in-betweens, unless you have the special skill of teleportation...and most of us don't! A lot of us often schedule ourselves so tightly that we barely account for travel time, never mind traffic and forget about parking!

Schedule it all, because it all takes longer than we think. And it creates great stress and tardiness.

Little Thing #99

Time takes time!

If you are on time you are 5 minutes late! It seems to me in this day and age we are all trying to squeeze 30 hours into our 24 hour schedules and life! And we are in a constant state of not being present because we are thinking about where we need to be or where we are supposed to be. Or worst yet, making up reasons and excuses for why we are not where we said we would be!!!

One of my counselor friends once shared with me, that *if I only knew* the kind of physiological damage that goes on in my body with the stress that happens when I run late, I would *never* do that to myself!

Give yourself the gift of showing up 5 minutes BEFORE you are supposed to show up, and allow your molecules to catch up to you. Once you arrive, settle in, close your eyes, and meditate while you wait for your appointment.

This little thing, my friends is a huge Little Thing!

One Last Little Thing
Little thing #100

To thine own self be true

When you are really perplexed about the right thing to do. Stop. Check in. What does your inner self, the real you want and need? That is your answer. At the end of the day, you have to live with yourself. And if you have sold yourself out by not being authentic and true to the one you have to answer to, there are all kinds of dues to pay in consequences. So listen to your Little Voice, the answers always lie quietly, and sometimes not so quietly within.

So you see, at the end of the day, it is the many little things that we do consistently over time that can make our life an amazing and joyful journey. It's the little things that make a HUGE difference in our lives and the lives of those we love and care about! Doing the little things, and being happier, healthier and more joyful will result in you creating a resonation that will ripple out into the world and create more of the same!

Be joyful, healthy and happy, it is your birthright!

Disclaimer

This book was written with the expressed intention of entertainment. These tips are suggestions as ways to possibly improve our lives in small ways. It is not intended to heal, cure or treat any types of mental or physical health issues or otherwise. Before attempting exercises please see your physician to assure you are in condition to pursue the exercises.

www.ingramcontent.com/pod-product-compliance
Lightning Source LLC
LaVergne TN
LVHW021459080426
835509LV00018B/2338